WILD BIRDS

Beautiful

COLORING BOOK

THIS BOOK BELONGS TO:

CREATIVEBLOX
PUBLISHING

For Elijah

Creativeblox brand coloring pages are created by a team of international artists and illustrators.

Great Hornbill
BUCEROS BICORNIS

Brown-throated Sunbird
ANTHREPTES MALACENSIS

Blue Crowned Pigeon
GOURA CRISTATA

Hoopoe
UPUPIDAE

Channel Billed Toucan
RAMPHASTOS VITELLINUS

Flamingo
PHOENICOPTERIDAE

Gouldian Finch
ERYTHRURA GOULDIAE

ARDEA HERODIAS

Keel Billed Toucan
RAMPHASTOS SULFURATUS

Hyacinth Macaw
ANODORHYNCHUS HYACINTHINUS

Javan Banded Pitta
HYDRORNIS GUAJANA

Silver-Breasted Broadbill
SERILOPHUS LUNATUS

CALOENAS NICOBARICA

Quetzal
PHAROMACHRUS MOCINNO

Ultramarine Flycatcher
FICEDULA SUPERCILIARIS

Spangled Cotinga
COTINGA CAYANA

Atlantic Puffin
CYANOCITTA CRISTATA

Mandarin Duck
AIX GALERICULATA

Ring Necked Pheasant
PHASIANUS COLCHICUS

Mountain Bluebird
SIALIA CURRUCOIDES

CEYX ERITHACA

Kingfisher
ALCEDINIDAE

ACRIDOTHERES GINGINIANUS

Golden Pheasant
CHRYSOLOPHUS PICTUS

Common Green Magpie
CISSA CHINENSIS

Orange-Breasted Trogon
HARPACTES ORESKIOS

European Roller
CORACIAS GARRULUS

Scarlet Ibis
EUDOCIMUS RUBER

Wood Duck
AIX SPONSA

Emerald-Bellied Puffleg
ERIOCNEMIS ALINE

www.ingramcontent.com/pod-product-compliance
Lightning Source LLC
Chambersburg PA
CBHW081247250726
48654CB00012B/1509